THE DEATH OF KING JOHN

A play by

Peter Tyrer

A play to mark the 800th anniversary of the death of King John in Newark Castle

ISBN: 153943270X
ISBN-13: 978-1539432708

OTHER TITLES FROM BLUE FROG PUBLISHING

Struggling Up The Hill by Robbie Taylor

Poetry From The Pub by Lincoln Writers Collective

Hitchcocks Baby by Steve Cawte

Insert Suitable Title Here by Steve Cawte

The Moon Belongs To Christopher Becker by Robbie Taylor

The Age of Jack by Robbie Taylor

Blue Frog Publishing is an East Midlands-based publishers for more information contact bluefrogpublishing@gmail.com

Introduction by Professor Peter Tyrer

King John is considered by most commentators to have been a bad king, or even worse, a bad and evil king. It is difficult to make any new judgments 800 years after his death without new information and so any verdict in 2016 is bound to be speculative. But there are good reasons for history to be a little kinder to John than it has been in the past. Certainly the view of Matthew Paris, a chronicler of the age, could not have been more negative, 'Foul as it is, Hell itself is defiled by the fouler presence of John'. But of course, John was unpopular with everybody. It used to be said of all kings in England that they remained popular as long as they did not raise taxes, and John was the champion taxing king, mainly because he lost so many battles and so did not win any of the spoils.

The events in this play take place in the last eight days of his life and they give some clues about his attitudes and state of mind at this time.

What is clear from every account is that in October 2016 here was a King on his beam ends. Half the country was occupied by French troops supporting rebel barons, the national finances were in free fall, he had lost most of his inherited possessions in France, his wife was fed up with his dalliances with other women, and he could not count on anyone as a friend. This was hardly surprising; he was stout, unattractive, spiteful, generally nasty and vindictive, and nowadays he would be regarded unequivocally as having a personality disorder. In many ways he was rather like Adolf Hitler in the last days of the Third Reich, with the country and economy in ruins and the fabric of the nation falling apart.

So how was it, in these last eight days of his life that King John was able to avoid an ignominious death like Hitler's in the Berlin bunker, have a solemn and dignified burial, and bequeath a stable legacy to the nation with a successor as King of England, his son, Henry, who ruled for the next 56 years?

The reason lies in the better and less well-known aspects of John's personality and his sense of history. Despite his failings in battle and inability to make friends, he was an able administrator and had the ability both to plan ahead and keep accurate records of his administration.

Indeed, he started early while his brother, Richard the Lionheart, was King of England. Richard earned plaudits for his derring-do in the Crusades but the government in England still had to function, and Prince John took on this task and did it pretty well. When he became King he also took his legal and administrative responsibilities seriously, and often took part in judging the merits of appeals made by his countrymen when they felt they were treated unfairly. So it seems a little unfair that he is mainly remembered for signing the Magna Carta at Runnymede under duress, when at that time he was mainly concerned with rebel barons taking over the country and removing him altogether.

So when John became ill after travelling from King's Lynn in Norfolk on 12th October he was not in the mood to throw in the towel. He was originally planning to outflank the French and rebel troops in Lincoln by a rapid movement north but had to abandon this when his baggage train got stuck in the Wash. When he became ill, probably with dysentery, he did not just take to his bed and let others get on with governing the parts of the country still under his control. He wrote letter after letter to other nobles and barons across the country, promising them land and money if they rallied to his side. The recipients all realised he had no money to give, but the land was an attraction.

So all this must have been going through his head as he travelled in a litter along the bumpy road from Swineshead to Sleaford, and then north-east via Leadenham to Newark, probably arriving to Newark Castle along the road that is now Northgate. It must have been a miserable journey, especially considering the pestilence in his bowels, but it gave John plenty of time to ruminate on where he had gone wrong in life. So it is not at all surprising his speeches in the play are misanthropic and so full of self-criticism and doubt. With so many things going wrong in his life he must have been assailed by guilt and blame.

It is not difficult to guess what was going on in his mind. 'Why did I have to spend so much of my time fighting battles in places where I could never win? Why did nobody trust me? If I had avoided all this conflict I would not have needed to tax my people to the point of penury, and would then might I have been less hated?' This was probably the first time in his life that he had time to reflect without being interrupted, and, with death expected rather than battled against, he must have been imbued with a pervading sense of gloom. In spite of all this, he was still looking ahead to the future of his realm and the destiny of his household, and so his flow of correspondence continued right up to his death. He was most prolific when ensconced in Newark Castle, particularly after he rallied a little (following what the play suggests is Dr Colman's intervention), and wrote letter after letter on 17th and 18th October exhorting all his correspondents to join in the struggle to restore him to his rightful place as King John of England, Ireland and Acquitaine, with his throne in London. They were not to know that he would never be able to honour any of his promises.

John's sense and awareness of history also helped his last days. He knew his son, Prince Henry, was next in line to the throne. Indeed, he had ensured it by getting the only other contender, Prince Arthur, murdered in Normandy many years earlier, and all those round the King were aware that the succession needed to be sorted out quickly after he died. Although few people were close to John, he did have two loyal stalwarts, William Marshal, an impressive battle-hardened General in his army, and Baron Hubert de Burgh, who stayed with him solidly from 1202 onwards. Both were instrumental in driving the French out of England, and William Marshal, despite being over 70 years of age, led the forces that defeated the rebel barons and French troops in Lincoln in 1217, acted as guardian for the young King Henry IIIrd, and restored Magna Carta to the law of the land.

So in a curious way, John's death smoothed the way for a more harmonious time in England's history. When he was no longer around, all the petty animosities he had generated over the years were forgotten, and Henry, being only 9 when he was crowned, had a completely clean sheet. Perhaps John himself realised this in his last days in Newark Castle. He understood he would not be well regarded by history but did his best to move the crown forward, satisfied that he had worn it for a time rather uneasily, but at least kept its continuity. The evil he had done should not live after him, and the honour of the throne should not be sullied. This is perhaps best expressed in the play in his last words:

'And high from Newark's walls please let this message ring

He served God and nation, and was a loyal, if imperfect, king'.

Imperfect he doubtless was, but all of us are too, and his faults were exposed bright and clear, in stark contrast to his almost subterranean hidden virtues.

The Death of King John

Dramatis personae (in order of appearance):

Peasants of Middle England
Narrator
Cuthbert, the King's cobbler
WlliamLongsword, bastard half-brother of the King
Leofric and Alfred –monks at Swineshead Abbey
Isabella of Angouleme, Queen of England
Walter, Abbot of Swineshead Abbey
King John, King of England and Acquitaine
Athelstan &Morgen – victual monks at Swineshead Abbey
Chorus of nuns at Swineshead Abbey
Agatha, the Bishop of Lincoln's niece
Hugh of Wells, Bishop of Lincoln
Messenger to the Bishop of Lincoln
Cedric, a Newark burgher
Tristan, another Newark burgher
Anne Beaufort – lady in waiting to Queen Isabella
Dr Colman, a physician of Newark
Arabella, Cook at Newark Castle
Bandolf, the King's personal servant
Wat and Nott, tax collectors for the King
Lady Faulconbridge, noblewoman in King John's court
Matilda, daughter of Arabella, the cook
Prince Richard, son of King John
Princess Isabella, daughter of King John
Prince Henry, son of King John and heir to the throne
Princess Joan, daughter of King John
Deacon of Newark
William Marshal, a General in King John's army

Act 1, Scene 1.

The entrance to Swineshead Abbey, Lincolnshire

(Peasants and denizens of Middle England, the forgotten backbone of the nation – stonemasons, scythers, builders, farm labourers and their children, cross the stage to be followed by the monks of Swineshead Abbey, who chant)

Narrator: It is the 12th October in the year of our Lord, 1216. The King of England is fighting his enemies in Lincolnshire, and, believe me, he has many enemies, not just in Lincoln but across the country and abroad. Although he has been on the throne for 17 years he has never reigned secure. Some people are troubled throughout their lives by agues and aches; King John is troubled by a much more serious affliction, barons. Like agues and aches, they never cease to batter his constitution and his health. A year earlier he has been forced by these assailants to sign a document, the Magna Carta, that took away many of his powers. Here was a man, ordained by the Pope, with a divine right to rule, having to sign a document including the words 'No free man shall be taken and imprisoned or dispossessed or outlawed or exiled or in any way ruined, nor will the King go and send against him, except by the lawful judgments of his peers or by the law of the land'. What nonsense, what treason, what anarchy.

Worse, in his battles with barons, Scots, and the French, King John has now lost his most prized possession, his baggage train. In his haste to confront his foes in Lincoln, he has crossed the marshy wetlands of the Wash, and his baggage, his treasury, his precious kingly wardrobe, are now rotting in the estuarine mud of that preposterous finger of ocean pressed into England's side. He and his tired men now turn to the nuns and monks of Swineshead Abbey for refuge on this gloomy autumn eve. There is one man in his retinue who never tires of talking - Cuthbert the King's cobbler – please forgive his intrusion on this serious scene.

Cuthbert the Cobbler:

'I'm a cobbler in the Royal train
It is a unlov-ed post, I trow
But there's some joy from being low
As now I can only hope for gain
There is no further I can fall
And as I scuttle around each foot
They forget to keep their mouthes shut
So I hear the secrets of one and all

And already I have much to tell
The treasures of our nation's good
Are well and truly stuck in mud
So the kingly train is far from well
The Lincoln folk all stand and stare
To the deep John's bestowed his baggage

From ermine robes to Royal cabbage
He has nought to eat and nought to wear'

(William Longsword walks to the entrance)

First monk, Leofric: Halt, who goes there?

William Longsword: Silence, varlet. You are in the presence of your King

Leofric: Kingly ye may be, but the evidence of my eyes tells a different tale. A more sorry group of men has seldom crossed my eyes

William Longsword: *(rushing over and pinning the monk by his arms)* you insolent monkish oaf, you dare to question the veracity of the King.

Leofric: Unhold me, sire. I am a man of peace.

Isabella of Angouleme: *(calling from the Royal train)* Please let us in. We need your help. We are exhausted. In the name of God, let us in. We indeed have the King with us.

Second monk, Alfred: Let them in. Charity must take risk without flinching

(The King's train enters and Walter, the Abbot of Swineshead appears from the Abbey. King John walks out and his manservant, Bandolf, shows the royal seal to the Abbot.)

Walter: I am satisfied. I have seen the Royal seal. We welcome you, Lord and master. Please excuse our misgivings, but 'tis a cruel world we live in and bandits roam the land.

King John: Would t'were different, I grant thee
A nation that embraced the warmth of healing balm
Where all could walk free from the shade of fear
And labour only for the common good
But for reasons that I do not fully comprehend
We have enemies within and without this realm
Who have sworn to bring us deep beneath their yoke
And though I feel the fight is failing in my feeble frame
While life's in me I'll not allow their gain.

Walter: Sustenance you need, and sustenance we will provide.
Come, we will restore your health in our refectory.

*(The party leave to enter the monastery, while some foot soldiers
tidy up the Royal train and prepare it for the morning)*

Act 1, Scene 2.

The refectory and barrel room in Swineshead Abbey

Narrator: The Royal party is now being revived by a meal prepared by the Swineshead monks, a simple dish of broth and beans. After the trials of the day this has all the appeal of the most delectable of banquets and the ravenous party could not be more pleased. But there is something missing - the wine. Athelstan and Morgen are preparing the victuals in the barrel room; meanwhile the monks hastily form a group to sing a welcome to the King to supper.

Cuthbert the Cobbler:

Greetings again from your cobbler true

I will have much to say to you

But your ears may now have heard my curse

My affliction is I talk in verse

So whether doleful low or joyful climb

My words will always be spoke in rhyme

But my eyes are sharp and hearing too

So I can show much that's kept from view

These monks are strange, not friends of King John

Methinks odd acts might be going on.

Athelstan: Well indeed. Did you ever think you would be waiting on a King when you woke this morning?

Morgen: There's no pleasure in that. A King who has robbed us all to keep his household in luxury. 'Tis something to be ashamed of, him stopping here.

Athelstan: I can't help but agree. Can't find anyone who will say a good word about him. He was called John Lackland when he was young, 'cos as the youngest son he wasn't expected to get any land or anything else, but 'e's certainly made up for it now, grabs anything he can get. And such a cruel man; they call 'im the hanging King 'cos he strings up all 'is enemies.

Morgen: Rage has racked the English throne nigh on 100 years. If tutored in violence, 'tis violent you become, so King John the Brutal is just bleeding from a common vein.
Come to think of it, just to show 'im, what say we give him that wine that makes everyone ill, from the barrel that burst. We've still got some left over in the bottom of the barrel.

Athelstan: we can't do that. Its treason to poison a King.

Morgen: It's not, and no-one will ever know. Nobody else knows about the rotten barrel. And in any case, who said it were poison. It's just special wine absolutely fit for a King *(laughs)*.

Athelstan: you convince me, but never say 'ought to anyone. We all know the penalty of treason is death, but preceded by torture on the rack - a stretch too far *(cackles)*

(Pours wine into an elaborately decorated flagon and fills the other flagons with good wine)

Morgen: *(as he pours the wine)*
O sweet and putrid wine your charms we sing
As we rid the world of an unwanted King.

(They carry a tray with the wine into the refectory, and as they do so the nuns break into song)

(Monks and Nuns sing to celebrate the King's arrival)

'Alleluja
Praise near and far
Your servants assembling
In fear and in trembling
O-Allelu-ja, O-Allelu-ja,
O Alleluja

Alleluja
Praise near and far
O Lord of creation
Bring peace to our nation
O-Alleluja, O-Alleluja
O-Alleluja'

King John:

Yes, peace again, on everybody's lips
If only a fragment was in my power
T'would be content to have this hand chop-ped off (waves left hand in air)
To bring peace again to this glorious realm
To see white doves in their soft and gentle flight
Instead of lowering hawks and falcons overhead
Preparing for the kill
But since that bloody battle at Bouvines
Bad luck has stalked me like an evil shadow
And brought me nought but woe
Defeat in conquest no joy can ever bring
Such decides the fate of every warrior King.

William Longsword: You deride yourself unfairly, sire.

Queen Isabella: No, it is not true. You have done what you have done, but not all life can be tragedy.

King John: I am not convinced. 'Tis the misfortune of a monarch to be reinforced by empty praise - but I will put my gloom aside while I sup. Good food indeed mollifies every excoriating thought. And I can also dull my doubt with good wine.

(He smells the wine)

A most unusual wine, but do my senses serve me ill. Do I detect the odour of the farmyard or the vineyard. Where does it come from?

Walter: Our cellars are famous throughout the land, sire. I can assure you of its quality. It is from your dominions in Acquitaine. Why not take a sip.

(King John sips the wine)

King John: (spitting out the wine) You 'sottish and ignorant monks. I'll not have this. Pour me wine from another barrel, and make it pure and sweet'.

(Morgen gets another barrel and gets ready to pour out the wine but adds a little of the rotten wine to the glass secretly before filling it up with the good wine)

King John: *(sipping the new wine)* Ah, a better glass. 'Tis sweet as nectar and will sooth my troubled mind

Athelstan: Tis pity such sweetness can be so unkind

Morgen: *(aside to audience – slightly mocking)*

We know not what will happen to our King

But we monks are innocent of wrong

We serve one master, the Lord of All

His caring hand will protect the meek

But not always the arrogant and strong

And we have only helped Him along

Act 1, Scene 3.

The Bishop's palace in Lincoln

Narrator: 'Hugh of Wells, the Bishop of Lincoln, who used to live in France, is in his palace at Lincoln. He has tried to make it a pleasant place to live, and as homely as his former palace in the vale of Wells. But has found it difficult to get used to living on top of a hill, with the wind howling in the winter. It is a constant struggle to keep the palace warm. He is also hoping to pay fewer taxes to the King. Although he is a loyal adviser, the King shows no favours when collecting from his subjects, whoever they may be. He would also be very pleased to see an end to the fighting. He is musing about the way forward to peace before he is suddenly interrupted by his niece, Agatha.

Agatha : *(niece to Hugh of Wells)* My lord and uncle, a messenger has given me this letter. He avers it is of great importance, and only to be seen by you, so I have brought it to you, tout de suite.

(Hands over letter to Hugh)

Hugh of Wells, Bishop of Lincoln: *(reading letter)* Oh my, the gods. The idiot loon. The nonnyingn ncompopple. The King has lost – a word scarce worthy of a blunder'd fool - his baggage train in the treacherous Wash. He is now in Swineshead Abbey, is far from well and asks for my help, hoping that I might align my cross *(fingers cross and points cross upwards)* in such a way to fashion a course towards health, virtue and redemption.

(Moves to centre stage)

A most trying sovereign I have to serve

Who when not scheming French adventures

Indulges in the strain of argument

Instead of conciliating calm

One constant theme has imbued his reign

Fight and lose, then tax and tax again

He's the nation's cat, acting on whim

Doing exactly what pleases him

And still, after every random crime

Expects to be fed at feeding time

Now he has enemies on every side

And we poor advisers meet shortened days

To preparethe path towards gentler ways

Thus now few places are left safe for him

But I know of one that will serve him true

Tell him that Newark will see him through.

(to Agatha) Tell the messenger to make haste to Swineshead Abbey, and to inform the Deacon at Newark to open up the castle in preparation for the arrival of the King of England – for, despite all his faults, he still deserves this epithet of rule.

Agatha: I will indeed. No time will I waste to ensure that this is done.

(shouts offstage) Messenger, in short time you must leave at speed. We need to send instructions to Swineshead Abbey and, in passing, to Newark Town.

Messenger: I seek to serve the Bishop, my lady, but Newark is not on the road to Swineshead and my horse is too weary to take the longer course.

Agatha: Away you scullion! A lesson in cartography indeed. Get thee another messenger as you will, but if the letters are not there by nightfall it will be the worse for you.

Act 2, Scene 1.

Entrance to Newark castle

Narrator: It is now the 14th October and dusk has come early to the town of Newark, a sleepy gentle town, nestling secure in a bend of the mighty River Trent, that long and sinuous watery snake that fattens as it wends its final pathway through the fens of Lincoln to the sea. The Bishop of Lincoln has indeed informed his vassals well at Newark Castle to prepare for the arrival of the King of England, warning them that his guts are groaning and will need a physician's help. The good people of Newark wish their monarch well - Royalists they are and Royalists they will be for generations to come. As the Royal party make their way up Northgate to the castle a scattering of townsfolk gather round as they enter the castle.

Cedric, a Newark burgher (shouting) 'long live the King'.

Tristan, another Newark burgher:

A worthy sentiment indeed, sir. But just at this time it may not be most apt. I hear the King has shortened the measurement of his life span considerably.

Cedric: you amaze me, and by what source do you speak?

Tristan: the Deacon of Newark has told me the King is gravely ill. And this must not be mischief as if we cannot trust and believe our holy men who in God's name can we believe.

Cedric: Sadly, such faith is a blind imposter. The world is full of artifice, even in the highest of the land, and I must needs rely on my own eyes for such rude awakenings.

Tristan: Well, look closely now, and you will have your answer.
(The King staggers into view looking very ill and collapses by the castle)

Cuthbert the Cobbler:

Yes indeed, the King is failing fast
They say his guts have turned to water
Spurting forth like Helicon's daughter
While his attendants just stand aghast
If the water fills his life is sunk
Drowned in his bowels will be his fate
But what has led to this sorry state
I fear he's been poisoned - by a monk

Chorus of Newark Castle staff
Lord and master, we thee honour
God in heaven we obey
Make our faith grow ever stronger
Save our souls on judgment day

Lord and master, daily feed us
Always be there by our side
Succour us and always lead us
Spread your goodness far and wide'

Act 2, Scene 2.

The Queen's bedroom in Newark Castle overlooking the town

Narrator: King John remains unwell. His court is sorrowful but not in despair. The King has always been far-seeing. He has made his plans for the future and all are agreed that the Royal succession is clear. Henry, his 9 year old son, the oldest of his children, will be king after John dies and everyone is relieved that this expectation is without dispute. A civil war is not about to break out; indeed, it would bring England to its knees. So Queen Isabella, still only 28 years old, has a future to look forward to with her five children. To tell the truth, she is not highly enamoured of John, whom she knows has been a rake and an adulterer, but he has been a fertile king. Better than Richard, his predecessor, who had shown he might have had a lionheart, but not a virile lion's body and was childless. It is pleasing that King John had made England fecund again. He could not peace produce but could at least can reproduce. So Isabella and her ladies in waiting, are not too displeased as they look over the battlements of Newark Castle to see the hustling and the bustling as people carry out their trade in the busy market square.

Queen *(sighing)*: Peace and Harmony do infill this town.

Ignorance of battle does them no harm

Not for them the rant and storm of kings

Squabbling over untilled barren lands

And wasteful of their countries' purse

Instead, busy with their daily tasks

In calm unhindered circumspection

Woulds't that I was so uniformly blessed

That I, like them, could join with all the rest.

Anne of Beaufort *(lady in waiting)*: Yes, the people of Newark do not concern themselves with affairs of state. You could say they have considered them very carefully, and have concluded they have better things to do.

Queen Isabella:

France and England; two proud nations forever locked in war, scrabbling and despoiling each other's lands like chickens in a pen, when each alone has plenty for its needs. Will there be no end to this pointless struggle?

And here am I, married to a fractious and fornicating king, whose eyes only see in me the promise of more land, land that he cannot even visit without an army, still less defend.

Anne: To the future you must look, my lady. The present and the past will soon be consigned to distant memory, and you still have youth and beauty in full array. Henry is a sterling lad, well fitted to take over the reins of government in due course, and, you never know, it may be sooner than we think.

Queen Isabella: You are right, my dear.
You take the correct and longer view
Whilst I rail at circumstance and fate
When I know I can alter neither
I should turn my gaze to fairer bournes
To my children's future in this realm
To times when I see destruction cease
And ploughshares take over from the sword
When good governance is there for all to see
Under Henry's rule, open, wise and free

Anne: *(looking through the window)*
Ah, I see a visitor. A person of repute, I trow. It may be the physician that the King so dearly needs. Let us hasten down below.

Act 2, Scene 3.

The entrance to Newark Castle, close to the Castle kitchen

Narrator: Dr Colman, a physician in the town of Newark, has responded to the message that the King is ill. Dr Colman is an enthusiastic physician, some might think over-enthusiastic. Sometime enthusiasm can overcome prudence, but prudence is not a quality you could ever ascribe to Dr Colman. He has heard from his friends in Newark that the King has arrived in Newark and that he is afflicted by an attack of dysentery. Now Dr Colman has a theory that he wants to put to the test, and who better to try it but on the King. So he has collected his thoughts, and some papers on the patients he has already treated, and comes with great confidence to demand an audience with the King. But he has to get through several barriers before he can reach his goal.

Bandolf: Aha, sire. What brings you here in such haste?

(Anne of Beaufort arrives)

Dr Colman: I understand the King is afflicted in the bowels. My craft is centred clearly on the bowels, and my enterprise on this day is to offer my good offices to his personage, though poor and scanty they may be.

Anne of Beaufort: Indeed, a bowel physician, and modest too. Perchance no doubt because your physick is deep below your fellows, who rise above you to treat the heart, the liver and the mind.

Dr Colman: You jest, my lady. But without good order in the bowels the mighty lose their strength, the valiant share only the mantle of the coward, and great thinking twists and turns awry to end in addle and confusion. The rumblings, burble and evacuations of the bowel may be mysterious and unimportant to you, but to me they cry out truth, rude health and inner peace when they rule in harmony. And if my hearing is correct, I understand the King is far from well within those oft unspoken regions of his frame.

Anne: So indeed, your stall is set. What can you offer our noble liege? You bind me with your oratory; can you bind his running guts as well?

Dr Colman: I can but try, my lord, and I have spoken already to the Abbot of Croxton, who has bled the King, and his attendants who have done what they can to ease the royal distemper. My authority here is the writings of that great physician, Hippocrates, the ancient Greek.

Anne: And what does this Greek offer our English King? A language check to challenge the Latin of your profession, a philosophy of the Muses, or a call to the diet of the Spartan soldier, a denial of all that has gone before?

Dr Colman: 'Tis none of these but you venture close. The secret of his problem is black bile, the humour that oozes out of his every pore. It has seeped into his mind, so he is bent on melancholy, it controls his stomach so retching out is more amenable than drawing in, and its prickling spurs have tickled and prodded his guts so much that they are afire. They twist and squeeze in agonising unison, and farting flatulent fluxions flow forth.

Anne: you intrigue me by your diagnosis, sire. But what is your solution?

Dr Colman: You are getting close, madam, in your suppositions. To remove black bile the body must abhor all that creates the bile - the flesh of bull and boar, the products of the sheep and cow, the beans and pulses of the fields. In short, only water must enter the entrails of the King.

Anne *(horrified)*: Only water! You wish to deprive the King of all sustenance. You wish him to waste away and drown in a sodden sacrifice to your fancy whim. I'll none of it. Our bold king is not a sponge, a shapeless mass deriving form from fluid alone, a dull wet rag to drop in casual caprice to smear the ground as you pass idly by. He has sinews, bones, muscles and a merry heart, and what good will your water cure do for these solid structures which in all their might make up the constitution of a King?

Dr Colman: I must correct you, fair lady. Water is the centre of our being. It soothes us like a soft and gentle cradle, keeping liver, spleen, heart, guts and, yes, even bone, in tune with all around. Without water we are but desiccated denizens of the desert, paper parchments like kites floating in the wind, with no direction save that decided by the elements. Who would wish this fate on any man?

Anne: 'Enough of this footling talk. You persuade me, sir. I do not know what you have in store for our good King John, but I cannot deny your conviction. Wait here a while, and I will see if he can spare some time to hear more about your bile notions in darkest ebony.

Narrator: The King is prepared to take any form of treatment that might cure his abominable dysentery and as he has completely lost his appetite the thought of water alone is not abhorrent to him. So he gives permission for Dr Colman to try his water cure. Dr Colman is pleased for this opportunity to show his outstanding clinical acumen and walks into the kitchen – but first he has to negotiate the formidable presence of Arabella, the Castle cook.

(Dr Colman walks towards the kitchen and is encountered by Arabella)

Dr Colman: Good lady, please abate your toil
Your work is not needed in this place
It now becomes the doctor's domain
Where the earthy mix of sustenance
Is transformed to the most pure of pure
The element central to our core.

Arabella: You joke in riddles, sire. Let me continue with my work. Speak clearly or leave at once.

Dr Colman: It is water, obtuse wench, to which I refer. Water alone must visit the entrails of our English king.

Arabella: And who are you, just a common thief
With intent to steal the skills I have
When I wish to serve our noble lord?
Or a charlatan on mischief bent
With dark thoughts behind those smiling eyes
Begone, thou pedlar of nonsense talk
Let me continue my allotted path
To prepare this king of pigeon pies
Its health and goodness strong and sure
So much better than your water cure.

Dr Colman: Waste not your empty scorn, peasant of the kitchen,
The King has approved my water physic,
And you must leave until I have gone

Arabella *(turning to Bandolf angrily)*: Canst this be true? Is my pie cursed never to grace the royal palate

Bandolf: Yes, cook of Newark, your pie must find a different home

The hungry of the town will strip it to the bone.

Act 3, Scene 1.

A room in Newark Castle

Narrator: The King has seen Dr Colman and it has been agreed that only water should be imbibed by the King for the next three days. The King indeed has showed some slight improvement and today is well enough to talk with his officers about his most favourite subject, tax.

(The King is meeting with his tax collectors, Wat and Nott)

King: What is the news about the people of Sherwood Forest? Have they continued to make no payments to the Royal Fund. Do not they realise we can no longer function in penury? Must I die a beggar while we cajole and chasten these dunderheads of Mercian malcontent. Have you recovered any of their money?

Wat: We surmised, and scrutinised, and theorised, but those elusive people of Sherwood are as slippery as a sizzling sausage. They jump this way and that and all seem to disappear into Sherwood Forest where none, not even the woodland denizens themselves, can find them.

King: Toleration is no longer mine to give. Retribution is the only answer, much as it disturbs my soul. Inside I am not an angry man, but sometimes anger squeezes forth and runs rampant till its task is spent. Tell the Sheriff he must reclaim 50 pieces of silver by the end of the month from this treasonous brood, or we will burn Sherwood Forest to the ground.

Nott: But is that not too hasty, sire. The wood is home to many in its glades and if they leave no tax can ever be collected.

King: (angrily) No matter how you do it, choose your way or mine, But please ensure you deliver it on time.

(Looks down at the tax receipts gloomily, then looks up)

Be off now, before I find another reason for distemper

(Wat and Nott leave in some relief)

King *(gloomily)*: The anger I show is born of fear
My fortune now an ocean of debt

Each tax I raise swells the country's ire

Bringing harm and threat from every side

So though I fulminate and bluster

Quicksilver tremblings run through my frame

A dreadful thought circling round my heart

A nation left bankrupt when I part'

Act 3, scene 2.

The Royal bedchamber

Narrator: It is two days later. We now enter the Royal bedchamber at Newark - where the King is beginning to realise that, despite the attentions of the good Dr Colman, he is really not improved and may die. He is now very weak, and the rumblings and explosions in his lower bowel have returned in full force.

Queen Isabella: you look troubled, my lord.

King John: I fear the worst; my body is losing the fight. I may not save myself; I only hope I can save my soul.

Queen: You distress yourself unduly, sire. A man who is battle scarred but strong, and still short of two score and ten, must be able to overcome this footling ill. And the people of Newark are praying for your recovery. More loyal townsfolk you could not wish for.

King:

I share not their hope, my mind is addled
Inspissated with morbid worms of thought
That my fever all too briefly doth suppress
Only to return in dreadful clarity,
The constant clamour of my misdeeds
In seventeen years since I first was King
How I failed to regain our Norman lands
And put Prince Arthur to the sword
When he and I were yoked by blood,
Hoping that each evil deed performed
Would be snuffed out by morrow's candle
And then return to triumphant day
But the light of morrow never came
And plunged into darkness again was I
Taxing and demanding more and more
Each battle dripping with our country's blood
And all seeming to be of no avail
But still I struggle, till I breathe no more
For the vision that still stands bright and clear
A land stretched from England to Acquitaine
A land free from conflict, harm and pain

(He sighs and seems distressed. Lady Faulconbridge comes to comfort him)

Lady Faulconbridge: Snuff out all ogrous thoughts, my lord, and let your rest be replenished by sweet dreams.

Queen Isabella *(talking to Anne)*

Yes, this vision is imprinted on his brain
implanted by his father at a tender age
And so I have no illusions of my role
Plucked from my intended at the age of 12
To add Angouleme to the English realm
What good has become of this? A tiny morsel
Land indeed but at what a price
With revolting barons and rebellious priests
No safe arbour beckons to my liege
And trust and loyalty are nowhere seen
A land more alien than my dear France
Where I would return but given half a chance.

(Sound of children laughing outside)

Anne of Beaufort: I trust the children are not laughing at those words, my lady. You remain Queen of England, a mark indelible never to be moved.

Act 3, Scene 3.

The nursery at Newark Castle.

Narrator: The Royal princes and princesses are playing together. Today, Matilda, the daughter of Arabella, the Newark Castle cook, has been allowed to play with them. This is highly unusual, but Anne of Beaufort has observed that Matilda is not only well regarded in Newark Castle, she has a distant relationship to William the Conqueror on her mother's side. She is well versed in languages and has an entertaining wit. Anne, being a very observant lady, has also noticed that Prince Henry appears to be fascinated by Matilda and is very keen to further their acquaintance. The King is ill and there is not much joy in the Royal Household so it is felt that Matilda may be an agent of good, so she has been invited, exceptionally, into the Royal nursery.

Prince Richard: We are all together now – it is time to dance.

(All the children form a ring around Henry in the middle and sing)

> **Prince Henry is dancing in the ring**
> **Fa la lalala, fa la lalala**
> **Prince Henry knows, he will soon be King**
> **Fa la lalala, fa la lalala**
>
> **Fa-lal-la-lal-lal-la-laaaa'**

(Matilda is now pushed into the middle and Prince Henry joins the ring)

Common Girl is dancing in the ring
Fa la lalala, fa la lalala
Common Girl is not worth anything
Fa la lalala, fa la lalala

Fa-lal-la-lal-lal-la-laaaa

(They repeat the dance pointing at Matilda when they say Common)

Common Girl is dancing in the ring
Fa la lalala, fa la lalala
Common Girl is not worth anything
Fa la lalala, fa la lalala

Fa-lal-la-lal-lal-la-laaaa

(Prince Henry gets distressed at Matilda being made fun of in this way and breaks away and goes into the ring with Matilda)

(They still sing 'Common Girl is dancing in the ring 'and Maud gets upset by the ridicule. Henry tries to comfort her and in the process gives her a kiss.)

Princess Isabella: He kissed her, he kissed her

Prince Henry: No I did not. It was a mere brush lightly on the face.

Princess Isabella: No, you kissed her, you kissed her.

Prince Henry: If I did kiss her, then I become a donkey.

(Children laugh and start a new chant)

All the other Royal children: Hee haw, hee haw, Prince Henry is a donkey
A donkey, a donkey. Prince Henry is a donkey.

Prince Henry: All right. So what if I did kiss her. Can a Prince kiss only those of noble rank?

Princess Joan: *(primly)*: We must do what we are told to do by our betters. We must not presume.

Prince Henry: *(putting his arm around Matilda, who is still up set)*

Princess Joan: Now you've kissed her you are going to have to give her some of your land, and after all, you are Lord of Ireland.

Prince Henry: Stop sisters - at once. This is a ridiculous pantomime.

Princess Isabella: No it is not. You started it by kissing her. At the very least she needs to be a Countess.
(She bows elaborately in front of Matilda, who is quite consternated and bursts into tears)

Princess Joan: *(jumping up and down in excitement)* I've got it, I've got it. With those flooded tears she has to be *(pauses for dramatic effect)* the Countess of Waterford. *(All laugh except Henry and Matilda)*

(Matilda is now very distressed and Henry takes her away to comfort her and before long they are engrossed in conversation)

Cuthbert the Cobbler:

'They will blink and splutter when I tell

What strange events have crossed my eyes

A young man and future king besides

Bewitched indeed by a Newark belle

These things do not happen in our realm

Nobles even to a cobbler bow

Is that going to be our future now

When we have King Henry at the helm?

Prince Henry: *(coming back to take control)*

Now it is settled. All will now form a ring and sing these words,

> **All now dancing round the ring**
> **Fa la lalala, fa la lalala**
> **Are equal when I will be King**
> **Fa la lalala, fa la lalala**
>
> **Fa-lal-la-lal-lal-la-laaaa**

All sing:

All now dancing round the ring
Fa la lalala, fa la lalala
Are equal when I will be King
Fa la lalala, fa la lalala

Fa-lal-la-lal-lal-la-laaaa

Anne of Beaufort: *(rushing in on account of the noise)* What a noise. Do not you understand. The King is gravely ill. All must be quiet in the Castle.

(All leave)

Act 3, Scene 4.

The Kings bedchamber

Narrator:

King John has now reached the point at which death is preferable to life. His guts are constantly groaning and groping. He realises that neither Dr Colman nor any other physician can do any more to help. He also realises that the country is in a parlous state, half occupied by Prince Louis and the French army. London, his seat of government, is occupied and still surrounded by rebellious and revolting barons who will only cheer his demise. He is miserable and depressed, and the full realisation of the troubles of his reign are at last bearing down on him.

He calls Bandolf into his bedchamber high up in Newark Castle.

King John: I feel I have let the country down. Do you not agree, Bandolf? Honestly I ask you to speak, as in my last days I cannot rest with cant and flattery

Bandolf: *(embarrassed as this is not normal behaviour for the King)*: you have served the country well, my Lord. It is not right for me to question those who are so high above the common people of this realm.

King John: but you have seen me through joy and ill
Witnessed the unfolding of my fate
How every triumph has turned to dust

Within the time span of a flower
Bright bud to bloom and then fast to fade
A chimera passing in an hour
And if I look closely at myself
I find the architect of folly
A man who failed to see the wider view
Chasing the goal of cheap advancement
Disdaining magnanimity
So petty and partial have I been
And left others puzzling in my wake
Knowing little of the King they serve
A man inclined only to offend
In troth, never have I had a friend

Bandolf:

I must contradict you, my noble liege
Remember the landing at Pevensey
When thousands cheered your safe return
From the Norman reaches of your realm
Surely then you had a friend

King John:

Sadly not, 'twas not for me they praised
But for the office that I have held
John Lackland was hiding in the rear
John Lackland himself received no cheer

Anne of Beaufort (*entering quickly and tucking him in*):
My Lord, this is not the time to fret
But preserve your strength - and maybe forget.

Cuthbert the Cobbler:

Well there's a pretty state of things,
A doctor who's run out of rope
A feeble king who's lost all hope,
And a servant who his praises sings
Where stands a cobbler in this Castle keep
When those so high have stooped so low
And all who talk are full of woe
Who needs shoes when all have lost their feet

(*Anne leaves and Bandolf is about to follow, but as is closing the door the King calls out*)

King John: 'Come back, Bandolph, I am dying

Bandolph: No my Lord, you will survive.

King John: No, I will not survive.

Too long have I fought against the odds
And thwarted fate with sparks of hope
But I feel a languor drawing near
And know soon a journey I will take
Far past the sign of no return
To a dominion quite unknown
Except to all who have gone before

And so, dear Bandolf, I merely ask
To staywith me ere I travel on
But before I go please promise me
Tell the world the truth when I am gone

Though history may bequeath a tale
Of a blaggard and tyrant monarch
Who listened little and acted less
Only when impelled by circumstance
Please do remind them of a kinder self
A man who tried to do the proper thing
To preserve the essence of this island race
In both its choleric and its gentler hues
So forget the stench of this garret room
A stench I grant whose generation is mine alone
Think instead of a life spent in service for this realm
And high from Newark's walls please let this message ring
'He served God and nation, and was a loyal, if imperfect, King.

(King John dies)

Act 4, Scene 1.

Outside Newark Castle

Narrator: It is the morning of October 20th, 1216. King John has prepared well for his death. He has given clear instructions to all his courtiers and servants; his body must be taken to Worcester where he will be entombed. The south of England is still in the hands of rebel barons and the safety of the funeral train cannot be guaranteed, so the loyal city of Worcester will be his final destination. The Bishop of Lincoln is sad to hear this, as a dead king in Lincoln Cathedral would be an enormous asset to his diocese. So he has hastened to Newark to find out if there is any doubt about the direction of the funeral train. The word of the King's death has spread through the town.

The people of Newark are also in mourning. They will not allow the Royal party to leave without paying their own tributes. He has been a taxing king, but not a bad one, and their last respects need to be proper ones. So a large crowd has clustered around the entrance to Newark Castle and the Bishop struggles to find a way through.

Hugh of Wells *(to the Deacon):* I have come to be appraised of the plans of the Royal household. Is the King going to be taken to Worcester or does Lincoln beckon as his final resting place?

Deacon: No. The King, as assiduous to detail in death as he was in life, has decreed that his body must be taken to the cathedral at

Worcester. There is absolutely no doubt; it is to Worcester that he must go.

(Arabella, Matilda and the other denizens of Newark castle assemble outside the castle to say farewell.)

Cuthbert the Cobbler:

Rain and hail, what storm came in the night
Newark vexed by the death of its king
Or the heavens parting as they bring
A troubled soul away from our sight?
But morning's here and new pleasures meet
As our Prince Henry will soon be crowned
And I for one will my praises sound
For at least he will have smaller feet

Arabella: *(still annoyed with Dr Colman)* Water indeed. If only I had been allowed to give him my good Newark pigeon pie with suet to bind up his bowels, our King would be alive and well today.

Matilda: Mother, fret not. It is done, and no-one can bring him back.

Arabella: And who are you, young lady, to give me such words of wisdom? Have you been gossiping with a sage, a knave, or a buffoon?

(Prince Henry, now King Henry III, comes out of the Castle with Prince Richard and princesses.)

King Henry III (to Matilda):

The time comes for me to say goodbye
Before I leave some words need I to say
Newark has brought such sweet sorrow
For though sadness fills my heart today
The joy of meeting you has tempered grief
 As these have been the happiest days
Of my curious and disrupted life
Filled a void where absence was before
And shown plainly that my father's court
Is no mirror of humanity
Its those like you who are England's pride
The ones to whom I must pledge my troth
No matter what else becomes my plan
I must ne'er forget the common man

Matilda: My thanks to you are a thousand fold

For you have shown me true charity

As the daughter of a humble cook

Expecting only a nodding glance

You have filled my heart with so much more

And emboldened me to stake a claim

To be the one who will most sing your praise

Now, and every morrow, all my days.

(They embrace, and then King Henry joins the funeral train)

Deacon: *(handing scroll to messenger)*
Go in haste to tell them at the fair town of Worcester to prepare for the arrival of a sovereign. A sovereign who will come but never, ever leave.

Messenger: Sire, be assured that your command is also now mine own. I will be there well before nightfall.

(The messenger leaves at a gallop, all around sing as the train slowly leaves the Castle on its route south to Worcester. All then sing)

He's breathed his last, his life is done
So ends the reign of our King John
Now the mantle will be taken by his son
To continue the fight until it's won
Yeomen fighting side by side
With Magna Carta to be our guide
England again will be strong and free
So raise three hurraaaaghs for King Henry
So raise three hurr-aaaaghs for King Hen-reeeeee

William Marshal: The rain clouds lift, we now greet new dawn

To cleanse away the stains of the past

With Prince Henry we breathe new hope

Into the fortunes of our realm

King John is dead, but the line of kings

Must stretch smooth and endless 'cross the years

Each tied to each by kinship and blood

But we must rein in the Horse of State

No more can we let a King untethered

Bend the country to a single will

So Magna Carta must be restored

And all who live in this glorious isle

Should hold these words in comfort at their core

None so high as to be above the law

END

The Death of King John - postscript

From almost the first day after King John's death, things began to look up for him, for his court, and for his kingdom.

Just before his death, John, whose administrative flair never left him, dictated a will. This still survives and is often displayed in the library of Worcester Cathedral. In this document John requested: "I will that my body be buried in the church of St. Mary and St. Wulfstan of Worcester". His body left Newark on the 19th of October and was transported the 110 miles to Worcester over the next four days. He was buried in Worcester Cathedral on 27[th]October, 1216, where his mausoleum still stands. When his body was exhumed in 1797, it was noted that he had been buried in a damask robe and wearing gloves with a sword in his hands.

William Marshal, almost certainly correctly, felt that to delay the coronation of the new king would leave a vacuum in government that could lead to unrest, so he organized the coronation of Henry III on the next day, 28th October, at Gloucester Abbey. Later, in Bristol on 12th November, Marshal was named by the king's council (the chief barons who had remained loyal to King John in the first baron's war) to serve as protector of the nine-year-old king and regent of the kingdom. He also made the astute decision to reissue Magna Carta to emphasise the dual responsibilities of monarch and people, and by so doing, enshrined Magna Carta for perpetuity in the laws of England.

But William had not quite finished. He still had the responsibility of getting the French invaders off English soil, and, even though by then he was 70 years old, this tough general led the English army at the Battle of Lincoln on 20th May, 1217 and defeated the forces of Prince Louis of France. The French were finally defeated in a sea battle off the coast of Kent on 24th August 1217. Marshal was generous in the surrender terms that he agreed with Louis in September 1217; but although some said he could have been more harsh, he was determined to have a period of stability for the young king to find his feet.

But what of The Queen?

Queen Isabella was less interested in the future of her eldest son. She was always much happier in France than in England, and returned there within four months of John's death. She did attend Henry's coronation on 28 October 1216, where she allegedly lent him one of her 'chaplets' (a garland for his head) but as she had been given no role in government she was excluded from the regency council and understandably was aggrieved.

So, in 1217, Isabella left England for her native Angoulême, ostensibly to escort her eldest daughter, Joan, to her chosen bridegroom, Hugh the Tenth of Lusignan, a powerful French nobleman. This began one of the most bizarre events of the time. Hugh originally was planning to marry Isabella herself in 1200, but John suddenly appeared on the scene, became infatuated with Isabella, and stole her from Hugh to be his Queen. This led to the entire de Lusignan family rebelling against the English king, and they never forgot.

So when Isabella accompanied Joan to plan her marriage to Hugh, she had something up her sleeve. She was much more fond of Hugh than she had been of John, and so decided to switch places with Joan and marry Hugh herself. The couple married in 1220. But there were other repercussions. Isabella's new marriage threatened the interests of the English crown. Isabella's alliance with Hugh had created a set of lands in southwestern France that John had coveted in Poitou, and now these might be lost.

After her marriage in 1220, wrote a letter to her young son, King Henry III, still only 13. This letter was an odd justification for her actions. She made out in this letter that Hugh's 'friends' were bothered by Joan's youth – she was still only 10 years old at this time – and had been encouraging him to seek another wife who was old enough to bear him an heir. But there was already one on the spot – Isabella herself, what could be better? So she married Hugh and insisted in her letter to Henry that 'we did this rather for your benefit rather than our own'. Others may detect a different motive, and we do not know if Henry was taken in.

To make matters worse, Isabella and Hugh then refused to return Joan to her brother in England. Instead they effectively kept her as a hostage, and placed pressure on Henry's government to acknowledge their claim to certain estates that had originally been promised to Isabella by John. Joan eventually was returned to England and married Alexander Second of Scotland in 1221, at York, becoming Queen of Scotland.

Queen Isabella died in 1246, but not before she had given birth to nine other children to swell the de Lusignan clan.

Hugh de Wells, Bishop of Lincoln

Hugh remained a highly active bishop in the Diocese of Lincoln. He also served as a royal judge in Lincolnshire, Nottinghamshire, and Derbyshire in 1218 and 1219. Later, he was asked by King Henry III to be an ambassador and negotiate with King Louis over the future of Normandy and, further south, Poitou, where of course Isabella was still active. Hugh was also credited with the creation of 300 new churches and vicarages within the diocese, but it seems many of these were 'refoundings' of churches that had pre-existed. But you just need to look at the villages of Lincolnshire and Nottinghamshire to realize that these numbers are not fanciful. There are still over 200 churches in the two counties. Hugh was also an able administrator, worked hard to improve the conditions of the poorer clergy in his diocese, and left a thriving legacy. When he died in 1235 he left his main possessions to his niece, Agatha.

Henry III

Henry's long reign of 56 years started well as he was not responsible for making major decisions. He also inherited some of the viciousness and spite of his father, and his French adventures lost more land and increased national debt. He also was not good at implementing Magna Carta, and like his father before him, aroused antagonism to the point of war. In 1263, led by Simon De Montfort, the Sixth Earl of Leicester, they launched a civil war against the monarch in 1263, and captured the King and his son at the Battle of Lewes. Simon established Parliament, until then simply a council set up by the king, as a proper representative body. This is the beginning of the rule of democratic nations across the world. With this power base, de Montfort ruled the country for a year until 4 August 1265. He allowed the King to escape, a major mistake, and subsequently Simon was executed as a traitor, but he was the first true personification of the principles of Magna Carta and the parliament he established is truly famous.

So the death of King John had far-reaching consequences, many of them anticipated by John himself, others created by his own personality deficiencies. He antagonized the de Lusignan family by his boorish snatching of Isabella, refused in his meanness to restore her lands even after their marriage, and ensured that at the time of his death his only allies were people who believed in the future of the monarchy, not any who were loyal to him as a man. These rebounded over time, and by the date of the death of Henry III there were even fewer French possessions in the English realm than in 1216.

But there were positives too. John, despite his differences with the strong-minded William Marshal, picked on William to be Henry's guardian, and so ensured a good early start to his reign. He also consolidated the monarchy by making sure his children had titles and important positions in the land. Richard, his second son, was involved in the crusades and eventually became an important European leader, but even he failed in his battles with Hugh de Lusignan. Joan, as Queen of Scotland, helped to keep Scotland in the kingdom, and one of his illegitimate children, another Joan, became Queen of Wales and married Llewellyn the Great, the revered Welsh leader. His daughter, Isabella, married Frederick II, Holy Roman Emperor, and improved relations with the pope.

Finally, Princes Eleanor, one of the most independent minded of the royal children, who was only 1 when King John died, was married to the son of William Marshal, also called William, when she was only 9, but he died 7 years later.

The final place in the royal merry-go-round was still to come. Eleanor fell in love with Simon de Montfort, the scourge of Henry III, married him secretly and had seven children, most of whom continued the parliamentary traditions of their father in supporting the substance, not just the words, of Magna Carta. So King John, in a curious way, not only created the basis of parliamentary democracy by abusing the powers of the sovereign, but reinforced it actively through his daughter.

If he was looking back on his life after 800 years, he might have concluded he did not do too badly after all.

Peter Tyrer, September, 2016

18327343R00037

Printed in Great Britain
by Amazon